A Note to Parents

DK READERS is a compelling program for beginning readers, designed in conjunction with leading literacy experts, including Dr. Linda Gambrell, Distinguished Professor of Education at Clemson University. Dr. Gambrell has served as President of the National Reading Conference, the College Reading Association, and the International Reading Association.

Beautiful illustrations and superb full-color photographs combine with engaging, easy-to-read stories to offer a fresh approach to each subject in the series. Each DK READER is guaranteed to capture a child's interest while developing his or her reading skills, general knowledge, and love of reading.

The five levels of DK READERS are aimed at different reading abilities, enabling you to choose the books that are exactly right for your child:

Pre-level 1: Learning to read
Level 1: Beginning to read
Level 2: Beginning to read alone
Level 3: Reading alone
Level 4: Proficient readers

The "normal" age at which a child begins to read can be anywhere from three to eight years old. Adult participation through the lower levels is very helpful for providing encouragement, discussing storylines, and sounding out unfamiliar words.

No matter which level you select, you can be sure that you are helping your child learn to read, then read to learn!

DK

LONDON, NEW YORK, MUNICH,
MELBOURNE, AND DELHI

DK LONDON
Series Editor Deborah Lock
US Senior Editor Shannon Beatty
Project Art Editor Hoa Luc
Producers, Pre-production
Francesca Wardell, Vikki Nousiainen
Illustrator Mike Phillips

Reading Consultant
Linda Gambrell, Ph.D.

DK DELHI
Editor Nandini Gupta
Art Editor Jyotsna Julka
DTP Designers Anita Yadav, Vijay Kandwal
Picture Researcher Deepak Negi
Dy. Managing Editor Soma B. Chowdhury

First American Edition, 2014
Published in the United States by DK Publishing
345 Hudson Street, New York, New York 10014

10 9 8 7 6 5 4 3 2 1
001—256581—June/14

A catalog record for this book is available
from the Library of Congress.

ISBN: 978-1-4654-2005-3 (Paperback)
ISBN: 978-1-4654-2004-6 (Hardback)

DK books are available at special discounts when purchased in bulk for
sales promotions, premiums, fund-raising, or educational use.
For details, contact:
DK Publishing Special Markets
345 Hudson Street, New York, New York 10014
SpecialSales@dk.com

Printed and bound in China
by South China Printing Company.

The publisher would like to thank the following for their kind
permission to reproduce their photographs:
(Key: a=above, b=below/bottom, c=center, l=left, r=right, t=top)
31 **Dorling Kindersley:** The Order of the Black Prince (tl)
Jacket images: Front: Alamy Images: Tim Gainey;
Dreamstime.com: Fxquadro/Vladimirs Poplavskis

All other images © Dorling Kindersley
For further information see: www.dkimages.com

Discover more at
www.dk.com

BATTLE AT THE CASTLE

Written by
Rupert Matthews

GUNNISON COUNTY LIBRARY DISTRICT
Ann Zugelder Library
307 N. Wisconsin Gunnison, CO 81230
970.641.3485
www.gunnisoncountylibraries.org

Missive 1

To Lady Eleanor, daughter of
Sir William Bekes of Horton
in the County of Kent

Greetings sister,

We have arrived at Oxney Castle. My master, Sir Edmund Perry, is being treated well by Lord Oxney. We have our own room in the West Tower. I even have my very own sack of straw to sleep on.

Our journey was tiring, but enjoyable. Sir Edmund was mounted on his gray horse, and I rode the pony and led the two packhorses.

We saw a man in a coracle fishing as we crossed the Great Stour River. Sir Edmund bought four fish for a ha'penny from him, and I fried them for our lunch.

We stayed the night with some monks at a priory. Sir Edmund slept in the Prior's house. I slept in the stable with our horses.

The next day, we left at dawn. On our way, we saw a huge pile of wood stacked next to a church. Sir Edmund said the priest would set the wood on fire if the French attacked. Then soldiers would come. Every town near the coast has a war beacon like this.

We arrived at Oxney Castle in the afternoon. It is a small castle with one large stone tower called a keep in the middle. Around the keep is a stone wall with smaller towers. Inside the wall is an area called the bailey. It is mostly grass, but there are several store sheds and workshops. Everyone is very friendly.

Squire's daily duties

A squire was a young boy serving a knight and training to be a knight. He would wake before dawn to start his duties. His duties included helping the knight get dressed and fetching and cleaning equipment.

MISSIVE 2

To Lady Eleanor, daughter of
Sir William Bekes of Horton
in the County of Kent

Greetings sister,

It has been three weeks since we arrived at Oxney Castle. We have been very busy because there has been a tournament!

Lord Oxney announced that he would hold a tournament on St. George's Day. He wanted to test the Oxney Array. The Array is made up of the local people who work for the king 40 days each year. Sometimes they repair roads or bridges, but most of the time, they serve in the army.

Sir Edmund was invited to join the contests for the knights.

There was a shooting contest
for the archers, with a huge prize
of 240 silver pennies.

The men-at-arms had to
run in armor from the castle
to the village and back again.

The women had cake-baking
and sewing contests. They had to
stitch a scarf with Lord Oxney's
badge—a white bear holding
a red sword. The winner was given
a whole bolt of Lincoln green cloth
—enough to make clothes for
25 people!

The contest for the boys, who set up tents and dig latrines, was very funny. A pig was let loose in a field. The first boy to catch it could keep it, but the pig was covered in grease. That made it very slippery, and I laughed so much, I cried.

Sir Edmund took part in the jousting. Two knights have to charge at each other on their horses. If one knight knocks the other off his horse, he wins. Knights also score points for hitting the other knight's shield, helmet, or body.

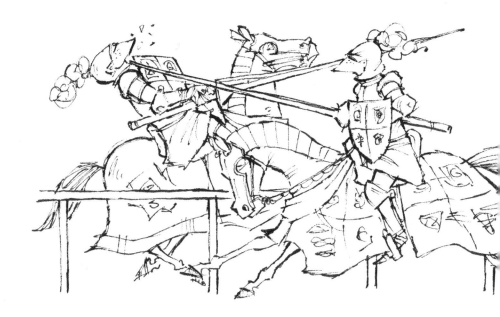

Each knight has a different pattern painted on his shield so that people know who he is. Lord Oxney's son, Sir Henry Oxney, had a white unicorn on a green shield. Sir Giles Black of Hythe had a yellow eagle on a black shield.

Sir Edmund took part in five jousts. He was not knocked off his horse at all! He scored five points, which is good. The jousting was won by Sir Giles Black.

Coat of Arms

In battle, it is important to recognize people at a distance. Most men wear helmets that cover their faces so every knight and lord has his own coat of arms.

MISSIVE 3

*To Lady Eleanor, daughter of
Sir William Bekes of Horton
in the County of Kent*

Greetings sister,

A French army has landed in Hastings! We received this exciting news three days ago. However, many local people are very worried. Lord Oxney is preparing to fight. Sir Edmund has been given command of 50 men from the Array. We have so much to do.

At dawn, the French army ran ashore, armed with swords and axes. They captured the Mayor of Hastings and made him pay 50 pounds of silver. They said they would burn the town if he did not pay.

Lord Oxney issued a
Commission of Array. That
means that all the Array must
come to Oxney Castle, bringing
their weapons and armor.

This morning, the French
burned Iden, which is less than
an hour's walk from here!
Sir Edmund told me the French
burn a village if the people run
away without paying money.

The people from Oxney have been coming to the castle. They are bringing their farm animals, money, grain, and farm tools. About 200 people are now camped in the bailey. They have built some wooden sheds to sleep in.

The people believe they will be safe here. They say the stone walls will stop the French soldiers. I hope they are right.

MISSIVE 4

To Lady Eleanor, daughter of
Sir William Bekes of Horton
in the County of Kent

Sister,

We are in great danger. You must help us. The siege is going badly for us. Let me explain.

A French herald came to Oxney Castle to ask for 100 pounds of silver. Lord Oxney refused, so the French army arrived and the siege began. We watched from the castle walls. We saw knights, crossbowmen, men-at-arms, men with spears, men with axes, and Baron de Gilles. The Baron had a coat of arms of a green dragon on a yellow shield. Beside him rode a man carrying a large flag with the green dragon.

On the third day, the French
brought up their two siege engines.
The ballista shot large wooden
bolts at the gate. Every time
a bolt hit, the gate shook, but
it did not break. The trebuchet
threw large rocks that went up
high then crashed down. Some
landed in the bailey, smashing
anything they hit. Several people
were killed. One stone hit the keep
and made a hole in the roof.

Lord Oxney told Sir Edmund
to destroy the siege engines.
That night, Sir Edmund led
his 50 men out of a small gate.

We crept toward the siege engines.
When we got there, we began
piling up bundles of twigs.
Then Sir Edmund told me to light
a fire. The French saw the flames
and attacked.

There was a big fight in the dark. Several men on both sides were killed. We carried our wounded back to the castle. Then we watched as the trebuchet burned, but the ballista was not destroyed.

The next morning, a terrible thing happened. The well ran dry. You know how dry the weather has been. The underground stream beneath the castle has no water in it. We have plenty of food and weapons, but we cannot live without water. You must tell father. Tell him we need an army to help us. I send this message in the hands

of a boy who says he can get over
the fence. God save us all.

MISSIVE 5

To Lady Eleanor, daughter of
Sir William Bekes of Horton
in the County of Kent

Greetings sister,

Good news! The siege of Oxney Castle is over. We are safe. Thank you, dear sister, thank you.

At dawn this morning, the lookout shouted for Lord Oxney. We all went up to the walls and saw Baron de Gilles on his horse, shouting orders. The Frenchmen were taking down their tents. They put on their armor and formed up in lines ready for battle.

Far to the north, we saw a great column of smoke from a war beacon.

The English army had arrived, and the King of England was with them. They drew up, facing the French with the knights in the middle and the archers on either side. The men on horseback were behind them. Then the battle began.

The English archers shot their arrows at the French. The French charged forward. There was a loud whistling noise as thousands of arrows flew through the air. All the French wore armor, but several were killed or wounded. The English knights were singing.

There was a loud crash as
the two armies met. We heard
the noise of swords hitting shields.
Men were shouting in anger or
screaming in pain.

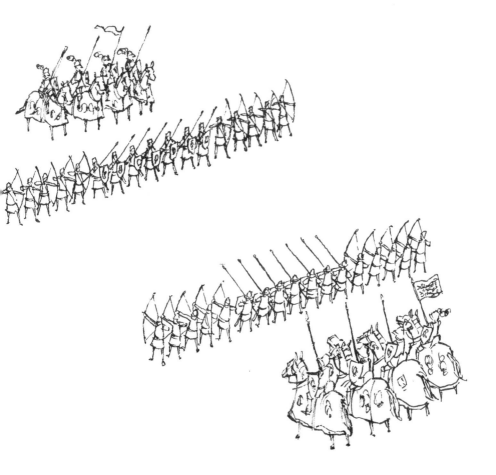

Suddenly, the French turned
and fled. The English horsemen
chased them, killing some and
taking others prisoner. Baron de
Gilles escaped back to his ship.
He forgot to take his chest of silver,
so the Mayor of Hastings got his
money back!

Lord Oxney says everyone
who was in the castle for the siege
will get a new set of clothes—
even shoes and underwear.
He is paying for it all. I am getting
a suit of brown woolen cloth with
brass buttons.

The King is staying here and
Lord Oxney is holding a great
feast to celebrate defeating the
French. I send you an invitation
with this missive. Please come.
Everyone wants to thank you for
getting the message to the King.

Castle Facts

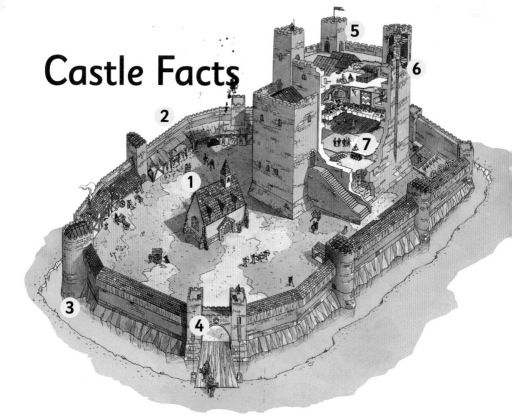

1. Bailey
During a siege, local people camp here for safety.

2. Walls
The stone walls protect the bailey from attack.

3. Moat
The moat is filled with water to make an attack more difficult.

4. Gatehouse
The gate is the weakest part of the defenses.

5. Tower
Men in the towers shoot arrows at the attackers.

6. Keep
This is the strongest tower in the castle. It is the last defense if the enemy enters the bailey.

7. Great hall
The Lord of the castle uses the hall for meals. Most of the castle staff sleep in here.

Glossary

ballista
a giant bow

bolt
medieval unit
of measurement
about 40 yards
(36.5 meters) long

coracle
small, round boat

ha'penny
coin worth half of
a penny

herald
messenger

missive
written message
or letter

siege
when an army
surrounds and
tries to capture
a castle

trebuchet
a giant sling

Index

DK READERS help children learn to read, then read to learn. If you enjoyed this DK READER, then look out for these other titles for your child.

Level 2 Space Quest: Mission to Mars
Embark with five astronauts on a mission to explore the planets of the solar system. First stop—Mars.

Level 2 The Great Panda Tale
The zoo is getting ready to welcome a new panda baby. Join the excitement as Louise tells of her most amazing summer as a member of the zoo crew. What will the newborn panda look like?

Level 3 African Adventure
Experience the trip of a lifetime on an African safari as recorded in Katie's diary. Share her excitement at seeing wild animals up close.

Level 3 Rain Forest Explorer
Through her blog, Zoe shares the thrill and narrow escapes as she travels through the Amazon rain forest to her Uncle's Research Station. What will she discover?

Level 3 Shark Reef
Blanche, Harry, Ash, and Moby are the sharks who live on the reef. Enjoy their encounters with the shark visitors that come passing through.